G000256917

AROUND
KINGSBRIDGE
IN OLD PHOTOGRAPHS
FROM THE COOKWORTHY MUSEUM
COLLECTION

MR DREW THE TAILOR with his apprentices, c. 1890. Most children left school at fourteen or fifteen and went straight to work. Many boys were apprenticed to local traders.

AROUND
KINGSBRIDGE
IN OLD PHOTOGRAPHS
FROM THE COOKWORTHY MUSEUM COLLECTION

COMPILED BY
KATHY TANNER

ALAN SUTTON
1988

Alan Sutton Publishing Limited
Brunswick Road · Gloucester

First published 1988

Copyright © 1988 Kathy Tanner

All rights reserved. No part of this publication may be reproduced, stored in a retrieval system, or transmitted, in any form or by any means, electronic, mechanical, photocopying, recording or otherwise, without the prior permission of the publishers and copyright holder

British Library Cataloguing in Publication Data

Around Kingsbridge in old photographs.
1.   Devon. Kingsbridge region, 1850–1974
I.   Tanner, Kathy
942.3'592

ISBN 0-86299-435-7

Typesetting and origination by
Alan Sutton Publishing Limited.
Printed in Great Britain.

CONTENTS

A KINGSBRIDGE GRAMMAR SCHOOL OLD BOY. Frederick Robert Elliot was tutor to the father of the present Duke of Edinburgh.

INTRODUCTION

In 1973 I moved down to Kingsbridge to work at the Cookworthy Museum and, happily, have been connected with it and the town ever since.

About four years ago the Cookworthy acquired a micro-computer as part of a project helping local schoolchildren to study local history. As a spin off, the Museum was able to catalogue and intricately cross-reference the museum's collection of about three thousand old photographs. When I was approached to prepare this book I was delighted – here was an opportunity to try out the searching capability of the computerised index – and I was impressed to find that it worked so well. However, even high technology cannot solve the dilemma of selection. Choosing around 220 photographs from 3,000 meant that I have had to omit many favourites. Sometimes whole subjects have been left out because there simply was not enough space.

Other omissions have been forced upon me. For example: cider was one of our major sea-borne exports. In 1808 Vancouver wrote 'Every valley throughout the South Hams is more or less occupied with orchards, which are much celebrated for the excellence of the cider they produce'. But there were no illustrations in the Museum's collections. Similarly, there are few good photographs of the celebrated South Devon breed of cattle, and none at all of anyone making our famous clotted cream.

I hope that the final selection gives a flavour of life in the South Hams during the last 150 years.

HISTORY

Today, this region is known to thousands who holiday regularly in the area, but in the nineteenth century it was still something of a backwater due to poor roads. Consequently, villages and market town had to be largely self-supporting. It had not always been thus. In Tudor times Plymouth and Dartmouth were two of the busiest ports in the kingdom and the rich farmlands of the South Hams helped to support them.

The name 'South Hams' is Saxon in origin and probably described the fertile meadows which must have been exceptional to warrant naming the region after them. They were certainly tempting to the Saxon kings who owned royal estates at Chillington (on the east) and West Alvington (on the west side of the estuary). There may have been a road between them which crossed the estuary at its northernmost point on a bridge – the King's Bridge. In 1086 the Domesday survey found no settlement near the bridge, but to the north there were two manors separated by a small brook called the Dod. To the east was the manor of Dodbrooke and to the west, Norton, centred on the village of Churchstow and owned by the Abbey of Buckfast. In the thirteenth century the Abbot created the new town of Kingsbridge on the hill at the head of the estuary. It had access to tidal waters, improving transport, and bringing the Abbot vital revenue from taxes imposed on markets and fairs. At much the same time the lord of the manor of Dodbrooke upgraded the cluster of cottages on his side of the Dod, granting them the right to hold markets and taking taxes.

Thus two towns grew up less than a quarter of a mile apart, each with a market, court, mill and shops. Over the centuries Kingsbridge dominated and finally absorbed Dodbrooke to become the market town for the South Hams, still a beautiful and prosperous farming region.

By the time these photographs were taken there was regular traffic between Kingsbridge and the villages, but even so, quite short distances seemed daunting. Pupils from Thurlestone had to board at the Grammar School because they could not get in and out each day. Courting was done 'within walking distance' after finishing work late, and Kingsbridge businessmen still holidayed at Torcross as late as the 1930s. As the extraordinary beauty and drama of our coastal scenery became widely recognised the economic balance began to shift away from farming and fishing towards the new industry of tourism. Some would say that these pictures show the last years of a self-contained community, but that is a romantic view of lives which had more hardships than rustic idylls.

In the second half of the nineteenth century the exciting new technology of photography was becoming more easily available and very popular. This book uses photographs taken by many local commercial photographers whose clarity of production and skill in composing a scene are still noteworthy. I would like to pay tribute to them (the dates come from trade directories): E. Calkin of Salcombe (working 1910 and 1914); E. Chapman of Salcombe (working in 1914); Balley and Flower of Kingsbridge (working at least 1901–1924); A.E. Fairweather of Salcombe (working in 1914 and 1926); Hammett of Kingsbridge (first quarter of this century); James Haynes and Mrs Sarah Haynes of Kingsbridge (working 1878 and 1889); W. R. Gay of Kingsbridge (probably last quarter of nineteenth century); Mr Ruth of Aveton Gifford (second quarter of this century); Thomas Partridge of Kingsbridge (working 1878 and 1889); S. Tope of Kingsbridge (working in 1889); B. Wyatt of Kingsbridge (working in 1910) and many others.

Most of the private photographers are unknown to us but one family is worthy of comment. The late Capt. William Beer, whose family had lived in Kingsbridge and Torcross for many years, left the Cookworthy Museum an excellent collection of albums and loose photographs. Unusually, they were not predominantly family portraits but illustrated people working in the area from the 1880s onwards. Some of the best 'action shots' in this compilation are from that bequest.

SECTION ONE

Farming and Markets

Kingsbridge was granted a licence for a weekly market in 1219. The area around the Shambles, formerly a butchers' arcade, used to be known as Market Place and was the economic centre of the market town. Even today, when tourism is a growing force, agriculture is still the most important industry in the area.

Until 1796 the pannier market (so named because produce was brought in on pack-horses) was held in a large Cheape House in the middle of the street. After its demolition the Saturday pannier market was held on stalls running down the east side of Fore Street from the Red Lion (89 Fore Street) to the shellfish stalls half-way down the hill. When the Town Hall was built in 1850, many of the butter and poultry stalls moved in under cover again.

KINGSBRIDGE 'MARKET PLACE',C. 1894.

KINGSBRIDGE'S LIVESTOCK MARKET was held in Fore Street until it merged with the Dodbrooke Market and moved to Church Street in the nineteenth century. The annual stock market associated with Kingsbridge Fair continued to be held in the streets into this century. This view was taken in c. 1900.

DUNCOMBE STREET, Kingsbridge Fair Day c. 1900. Traditionally, Kingsbridge Fair was a purely trading fair beginning on the Wednesday after the 'day of St Margaret' in July and continuing until Saturday. Today it extends to a full week with special events and entertainments, but there is still an animal stock market.

DODBROOKE MARKET PLACE in Church Street. c. 1890. Dodbrooke's weekly market and Quarterly Great Market were held at the foot of Church Street. In the eighteenth century the weekly markets were replaced by monthly ones and finally the Kingsbridge and Dodbrooke livestock markets merged. They were held at Dodbrooke Market Place until the new market was built in Ropewalk in 1922 (below – Major Luscombe is the auctioneer).

DODBROOKE CHRISTMAS MARKET. 1930.

FREE-RANGE POULTRY AT HALLSANDS, c. 1904. Fishing was a precarious livelihood and most families kept poultry – some also had allotments on the cliffs behind the village.

ROSIE TERRY of Kingston in her chicken run.

WESTON FARM, Yealmpton. Before 1914.

DUNSTONE FARM, Yealmpton. c. 1912.

SHEEP-SHEARING COMPETITORS and members of the Discussion Society at Lower Coleridge, 9 June 1927.

THIS AND THE NEXT TWO PICTURES WERE TAKEN IN 1925. The farmer, Mr Hooppell of Folly Farm, Bigbury, was conscious even then that the old methods were disappearing and he wanted to record them. Above: Mr Hooppell with a 'sillup' (seedlip) for broadcasting grass seed. Below: Using the scuffle to break up surface clods. It was also used for inter-row weeding.

BALANCE PLOUGHS like this were very popular on small, steep Devon fields because they left little ground uncultivated. At the end of each furrow the second set of share, coulter and mould board were swung down to the ground thus turning the plough to face the way it had come. They were made locally by Chamberlains, later Steers, implement works at Kingsbridge. A double furrow version is shown in Steers' catalogue below.

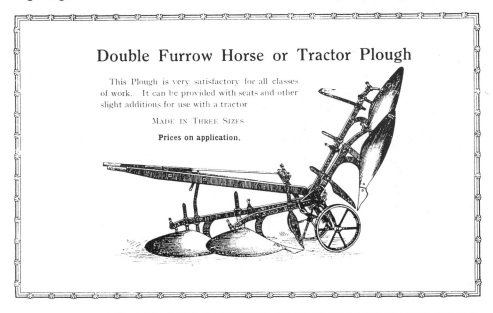

Double Furrow Horse or Tractor Plough

This Plough is very satisfactory for all classes of work. It can be provided with seats and other slight additions for use with a tractor

MADE IN THREE SIZES

Prices on application.

STOKENHAM, 1896. Before mechanisation lines of men with scythes used to advance across the field, followed by women collecting the corn into sheaves.

A DRAMATIC ACTION SHOT OF AN EARLY REAPER. The mechanisation of the corn harvest had a serious impact on rural employment. Early reapers merely cut the corn but later ones also bound it into regular sized sheaves and dropped them to be gathered into stooks (locally 'stitches' or 'shocks') to dry in the sun.

A TRACTOR-DRAWN BINDER ON COASTAL FIELDS. The reaper at the Cookworthy Museum has interchangeable horse-pole and tractor drawing bar. (Western Morning News, date unknown.)

STOOKING AT CORNISHES FARM, East Charleton. c. 1956.

BRIDGECOMBE FARM, LODDISWELL, 1905. Harvesting was a dusty, thirsty business; women and children brought food in wicker baskets and cold tea in a 'drinkings kettle'. When the sheaves of corn were dry, they were loaded onto wagons and carried to the corner of the field, or sometimes to a special rick yard. Rick building was a skilled craft – badly stacked or ventilated ricks could ruin the grain which was still within the ears. They were thatched with wheat straw for protection until threshing time. In rick thatching the length of the stem is exposed, unlike thicker house thatch where only the cut ends of the straw or reed can be seen.

THATCHED RICKS NEAR LODDISWELL, date unknown. Sometimes, small round ricks were raised up on stone staddles to prevent rats and vermin eating the grain.

A RICK YARD. Notice the typical South Devon style of farm wagon – they had to be light and manoeuverable to cope with the steep hills, narrow lanes and difficult field gates.

MR YABSLEY'S THRESHING TEAM. Few farmers had their own threshing machines – they had to wait until contractors came to their area. One of the biggest local contractors was W. Yabsley of Goodshelter, East Portlemouth. It took over a dozen men to operate a threshing machine and tackle. Notice the small cider kegs which provided personal refreshment in the field. Until 1887 part of labourer's wages were paid in cider, usually poor quality brew, the farmers keeping the best for themselves.

The grain was collected in sacks and the straw built into another rick to be used in winter for bedding. At the end of the last day the farmer would give a 'threshing supper' at the huge farmhouse kitchen table. A farmer's wife from Beeson gave their table and benches to the Cookworthy Museum with the comment that 'a couple of men from the combine harvester look a bit silly sitting at that.'

EDWARD HURRELL

H AS pleasure in announcing to Agriculturists that he LETS ON HIRE a Portable STEAM ENGINE & THRASHING MACHINE by *Marshall and Sons* and solicits the favour of their support which shall receive his best attention.

Terms : 2d. per bushel, and the customer to find the men Board and Lodgings.

The man in charge of Engine and Machine is responsible as to where he takes the same.

Further information on application to

EDWARD HURRELL,

or   BOWDEN;

Messrs. R. & W. HURRELL,

                BOWDEN;

1876

FOR SALE.

S AMUELSON'S COMBINED REAPING AND MOWING MACHINE, in good working condition. Apply to WM. PARKHOUSE, Auctioneer, Kingsbridge.

1876

YABSLEY'S AGRICULTURAL ENGINE, made by Charles Burrell and Sons of Thetford, which was used in threshing.

YABSLEY'S THRESHING MACHINE at Goodshelter, East Portlemouth.

Above: COLLECTING SEA SAND FROM MILL BAY, Portlemouth. Soils were improved by the addition of dung or lime, burned in kilns along the shores of Kingsbridge Estuary and the Rivers Avon and Erme. Sea sand was also used, mixed with mud and dung, while at Portlemouth, Chivelstone and around Bigbury Bay (below) seaweed was collected for use on the fields.

GEORGE SANDOVER OF WOOLSTON with the turnip cutter which he designed and patented in 1894. The basket beneath was called a 'maun(d)' – it could easily have been made by Mr Woodmason of Duke's Mill (see page 76).

A WEST CHARLETON FARMER tried growing flax for linen and linseed oil in the 1930s. The plants were sown close together to make the stems tall and straight and it was pulled by hand so that the fibres were as long as possible. The stems were then soaked in a pit to soften the fibre and dried in the sun for two to three weeks before being made into yarn.

FOLLY FARM, BIGBURY. South Devon did not have many landed estates so there were few official gamekeepers. These rabbits were probably shot as they escaped the reaper in the harvest field; or were there ferrets in those sacks?

THIS SHIPMENT OF RABBITS FROM KINGSBRIDGE STATION almost certainly came from the Tonkin Brothers, rabbit dealers, of Market Place, Church Street, Kingsbridge. They sent rabbits up to London during the First World War and until the late 1920s.

Kingsbridge Shops
and Inns

AN EARLY BIRD'S-EYE VIEW LOOKING UP FORE STREET. Hawkins, writing in 1791, described Fore Street as being sixty feet wide which is hard to imagine today. S. P. Fox, in 1864, described stalls which shopkeepers put out onto the pavement in front of their shops and it seems that this view shows the last remnant of those stalls, the lean-tos on the right. It was a simple matter for the owner to then rebuild the frontage of his shop on the new line, subtly encroaching on the highway and reducing its width.

THE PEARSE FAMILY outside the Seven Stars in Mill Street. One of the boys was later town crier (below).

DONOVAN'S BUTCHERS on the corner of Mill Street and Fore Street, 1920–30.

DIAGONALLY OPPOSITE DONOVANS WAS THE CORNER STORES. Behind it is an unfamiliar view of Duke Street before bombing in 1943. The archway at the end was the entrance to the foundry.

PRIVATE HOUSES AT THE LOWER END OF FORE STREET before 1878. The commercial heart of the town was up the hill around the Shambles. Mill Street and lower Fore Street were where the richer tradesmen used to live.

15 FORE STREET, KINGSBRIDGE. The Quarm family traded here from at least 1850–1910.

DONOVAN'S 'MARINE STORE AND CHINA DEALERS' had a shop in Church Street in 1878. In 1893 they moved into the old post office premises at 49 Fore Street and have been there ever since, the longest established family business in Kingsbridge.

61–63 FORE STREET, c. 1897. Stidworthy advertised that he sold glass and china but obviously had a good line in bicycles as well. These two buildings were bombed in 1943 and rebuilt.

THE SHAMBLES. 85 Fore Street. Behind the cart stood the Exeter Inn from the 1830s until 1935. The South Devon Brewery was behind the inn.

70 FORE STREET. There have been butchers' shops in and around the Shambles for over 400 years.

POST OFFICE AND DEVON AND CORNWALL BANK, Fore Street, Kingsbridge. The first regular collection of mail from Kingsbridge (via Ivybridge and Modbury) began in August 1798. The post office was always in the Post Master or Mistress's home until 1892 when this rather incongruous edifice was erected for that purpose. It was shared with the Devon and Cornwall Bank, previously the Plymouth and Devonport Banking Company which had opened a branch in Kingsbridge in 1832.

BUILDERS working on the Bank and Post Office in 1892.

95–97 FORE STREET. In 1882 Joseph Tanner bought a well-established draper's shop (no. 95) and the hatter's next door. His business thrived and in 1924 his son bought no. 99 as well. In 1986 Joseph's grandson and great-grandson moved the business to new premises on the Quay and this property is now three shops again for the first time for over 100 years.

'Where can you be supplied with any and every want better than in Kingsbridge? Where will you find butchers, bakers, brewers, vintners, tailors, drapers, druggists, grocers, booksellers, coal merchants, upholsterers, ironmongers, milliners, hatters – in short, followers of pretty nearly every known trade and calling under the sun, better able to supply the wants of the body and the longings of the mind than those who flourish in Kingsbridge?'

Francis Young, 1861.

THE ALBION HOTEL at the top of Fore Street in c. 1900. The Port family built this hotel in 1874 and sold it for £2,500 in 1894. On the 7 October 1898, the first motor car ever seen in town stopped there. The buildings to the far left have been demolished to make way for the upper car-park. Veysey Stoneman had a grocers and music shop side by side. Local schoolboys always called him 'Namenots' (pronounced Namminots – his name spelled backwards!).

THE PLYMOUTH INN, 129 Fore Street. The inn was already open by 1841 and closed in 1916. In 1896 this was one of the last places to brew 'White Ale', a noxious and notorious local liquor. It was made from malt, hops, eggs and flour with a mysterious ingredient called 'grout'. It was drunk very young, was highly intoxicating, and a local taste which few acquired in later years. (Devon Library Services)

9 CHURCH STREET. The building bears a plaque inscribed 'Market House 1885' after the Dodbrooke market which was held across the road.

AT THE FOOT OF CHURCH STREET the King of Prussia changed its name to the George to avoid anti-German feeling between the wars. Here it is decorated for the 1935 Jubilee.

COURT'S FISH AND CHIPS, Duke Street, 1920–30.

5 DUKE STREET (formally Duck Street because it was an open stream), Kingsbridge. This shop was destroyed in 1943 by enemy action and the site is now part of the Post Office yard.

RYEFORD GARAGE, The Quay, Kingsbridge. The Quay area has always been the centre of the transport system; first by water, later by road.

RICHARD WEST, carrier to Loddiswell, in front of Balley and Flower's studio at 99 Fore Street, Kingsbridge. Carriers used to go to the villages on particular days. On those days, or the day before, they would wait on the Quay to collect any parcels from Kingsbridge to the villages.

MR LEN GEATCHES of Kingsbridge served his apprenticeship as a wheelwright, making everything wooden from wheelbarrows to wagons, but he had to turn his hand to new skills. He helped to build the cab on this first covered tractor in the district in c. 1937.

89 FORE STREET, Kingsbridge. In the 1820s this was the Red Lion Inn where corn sales were held. Subsequently the Blackler family had an ironmonger's shop there for over eighty years. They also held agencies for agricultural machinery.

SECTION THREE

Around The Villages

At the turn of the century every village had at least one general shop and several had specialist bakers, butchers, shoemakers and other craftsmen. Villagers could get many things locally and most of the major Kingsbridge shops had vans which did regular rounds.

BANTHAM, c. 1892.

S. GILES, Baker of Salcombe, delivering to Malborough and Hope Cove.

JIM ROGERS, carrier, of Beeson at Chillington. The carriers would carry messages, undertake commissions and give lifts in addition to delivering goods.

WOODLEIGH'S VILLAGE SHOP AND POST OFFICE was in the other half of this thatched cottage beside the church gate.

JAMES WILLIAM KENNARD proudly displaying his postman's uniform in c. 1898. He was also the sexton at Woodleigh, and son of George Kennard, the Woodleigh blacksmith.

WEST ALVINGTON, C. 1892. In 1850 West Alvington boasted two blacksmiths, three carpenters, four masons, two plumbers, a shoemaker, tailor, baker and general shopkeeper. Most of these made a living from the village and parish, not commuting to Kingsbridge as today.

DELIVERY VAN AT LOWER TOWN, West Alvington.

MODBURY, LOOKING EAST. Although Modbury was officially part of the Kingsbridge Union from the nineteenth century, it was a purely legal distinction. It was an entirely separate community with few links with Kingsbridge. Indeed, the two towns almost came to blows during protracted attempts to bring a railway to Kingsbridge between 1856 and 1893. Eventually it was routed well to the north of Modbury, contributing to a fall in population which began with the decline of woollen manufactures here in the first quarter of the nineteenth century. Nevertheless, Modbury maintained its commercial prosperity as may be seen from the substantial town houses.

INNER HOPE in c. 1892.

THE PILCHARD INN, Burgh Island. The name reflects the importance of pilchard fishing in Bigbury Bay in the eighteenth and first half of the nineteenth centuries.

THURLESTONE VILLAGE. The village shop is now further down the street.

MALBOROUGH MAIN STREET. In 1914 Malborough had three shopkeepers, two carpenters, a shoe repairer, a blacksmith and a tailor.

SOUTH MILTON, Police Cottage.

THE MANOR OF CHIVELSTONE dates back to the reign of Henry III but it has never been a large or rich parish. Even so, in 1857, the village and parish supported a tailor, blacksmith and mason as well as a post office. The Seven Stars Inn, close to the church, was also popular.

Salcombe — from Bonfire Hill.

MERRELL'S SERIES. 179.

SALCOMBE FROM BONFIRE HILL. Today Salcombe is *not* a village, it is a town in its own right. It grew quite rapidly from the small fishing village which nestled under the protection of Bolt Head. Always a more important fishing and shipbuilding centre than Kingsbridge, the inhabitants still regarded Kingsbridge as a convenient market town.

SALCOMBE from above South Sands.

HANNAFORD'S Greengrocers, Salcombe, c. 1900.

SOUTH POOL. A Domesday manor, then called Pola. The title of Lord of the Manor persisted until at least the First World War.

MINGO'S SHOP, Hallsands. The isolated hamlet of Hallsands had a baker's shop and post office, the former run by the Mingo family for over thirty years.

THE LONDON INN at Hallsands was storm-damaged repeatedly between 1902 and 1904. On this occasion it was reported to have opened for business as usual.

TORCROSS C. 1890. Torcross has grown out along the shingle beach, the older houses finding secure footings on the rocky platforms at the southern end. The village was always vulnerable to storms and this picture shows an early sea wall. Severe damage in 1951 and again in 1979 led to more substantial defences. It is often said that the recent disasters were results of gravel dredging off Hallsands in 1901 which led to the destruction of that village; it will probably never be proved one way or the other.

This was a fishing village like Beesands and Hallsands. In 1864 a visitor recounted how the fishermen kept Newfoundland dogs which were trained to swim out and catch the ropes from incoming boats in stormy weather. They also brought balks of timber (called 'ways') to place under the boat as it was drawn up the beach.

THE FISHERMAN'S ARMS, Torcross.

DARE'S DRAPERY at Torcross c. 1900.

Quays, Roads and Railways

It was usually quicker to send goods by water than by road and Kingsbridge's position at the head of a long creek (not truly an estuary) was very important. However, by a quirk of geography, neither of the two main quays actually lay within the parish of Kingsbridge.

In medieval times the water probably came up as far as Mill Street and Duke Street. Over the centuries quays have been built out over the silting mudflats. The west bank of the estuary lay within West Alvington parish. It was the last to be reclaimed from the mud to create Square's Quay. On the east side, Dodbrooke Quay (below) ran southwards to the Salt Mill Quay and finally to New Quay.

Dodbrooke Quay, c. 1890.

LARGE VESSELS used to come right up to the head of the estuary to unload, c. 1870.

THE MEADOW IN THE FOREGROUND used to be another branch of the creek, with Salt Mill Quay beside it. Across the water is Square's Quay with logs waiting for the sawmill.

NEW QUAY, Kingsbridge, c. 1875. As the head of the estuary silted up, a new quay was built where the deep water channel came close to the eastern bank. Everything from fertiliser to cheese was unloaded here. (Devon Library Service.)

NEW QUAY was owned by the Bond family for several generations. This is Bill Bond on what came to be known as 'Bond's Quay'. (Picture 1910–11.) The family exploited the seamen's thirst and opened the New Quay Inn, now the Crabshell.

PASSENGER FERRIES from Plymouth and Salcombe used Bond's Quay at low tide. The *Express* was built by Dates of Kingsbridge and launched in 1885.

ON THE DECK OF *REINDEER*. Launched in 1875 she was flat-bottomed, drawing only two feet with engines, to navigate the shallow channels of the Estuary. *Reindeer* could carry 250 passengers.

FORE STREET TOLL GATE, pre-1884.

'The Waggon and Cart may be said to be wanting in the South Hams . . . . A Road Team I do not recollect to have seen, out of the public road between Exeter and Plymouth, and very few on it. Pack horses, I believe, are the prevailing, or universal means of transfer, whether of produce, of manure, or of materials in general . . . . I have seen building stone carried on horse back.' (Marshall, 1796)

Local lanes were so deep, muddy and tortuous that pack-horses were far more common than wheeled transport until Turnpike Trusts were established to improve roads in the early nineteenth century. To recoup their costs, charges were levied at toll-gates across the main roads.

Turnpike Trusts reached south Devon rather late and were dismantled in 1884. The two gateposts from this gate can still be seen in a nearby house's driveway.

DONKEY POWER.

ROAD MENDING TEAM near New Mill on the road between Loddiswell and Woodleigh.

THE DARTMOUTH COACH at Torcross. Stagecoaches ran from Kingsbridge to Plymouth from 1824 but the Dartmouth service did not begin until some 30 years later. A proper road along the Line, linking Torcross and Strete, was not fully opened until 1856 and the first coach service began soon after that. The main stages were from the Anchor Hotel (now the Quay) at Kingsbridge to the Torcross Hotel and thence to Dartmouth. At Torcross an extra horse was added to help get up the steep corner at Strete Gate. This was one of the last regular passenger services to operate, only ending when the coachman went to war in 1916.

A FORETASTE OF THINGS TO COME?

FORE STREET in the 1930s.

THE FIRST ENGINE THROUGH THE LINE WAS A WORKS ENGINE, seen here with the proud labour force. (Devon Library Services)

THE RAILWAY

It was 57 years after a Kingsbridge rail link was first suggested that it opened in 1893. When the last in a series of local companies was threatened with closure the Great Western Railway finally stepped in and completed the line from South Brent to Kingsbridge.

The line, designed by W. Clarke, engineer to the Great Western Railway, was just over 12 miles long and cost around £180,000. There were 48 wrought iron bridges and the line crossed the River Avon in ten places. There was also a 640-yard tunnel at Sorley. The four stations were at Avonwick, Gara Bridge, Loddiswell (Woodleigh) and Kingsbridge.

CONSTRUCTING A RAILWAY BRIDGE over the River Avon near Woodleigh. 1892–3.

THE OPENING OF THE KINGSBRIDGE LINE, 1893.

THE OPENING WAS CELEBRATED IN FINE STYLE, somewhat to the surprise of the Great Western Railway to which it was, by 1893, rather a commonplace event.

LODDISWELL STATION.

TRAFFIC FAR EXCEEDED EXPECTATIONS. In the first week the Stationmaster realised that the space outside Kingsbridge Station was totally inadequate for all the vehicles which came to meet the trains, and part of the bank behind the station was removed. Later, the station building was extended and more sidings were added.

THE DARTMOUTH COACH approaching Kingsbridge Station, c. 1900. (The Van Houten sign is now in the Museum).

THE PLANNED EXTENSION TO SALCOMBE was never built but there was a regular GWR bus service. Joe Foale, who ran the GWR parcel service until 1899, had previously driven the Kingsbridge to Wrangaton stagecoach which was put out of business by the railway. Joe (with straw hat) stands here, with Boxer Wakeham, beside the coach which took rail travellers to the Kings Arms Hotel.

VIEW OVER THE STATION FROM WEST ALVINGTON HILL. Postmarked 1910.

SECTION FIVE

Crafts and Industry

In the nineteenth century South Devon was not heavily wooded although coppice woodland was grown on the steep slopes of river valleys. Most large trees grew on the massive earthen hedge-banks. Timber was bought standing and, when felled, allowed to mature for many years before being used. There were sawmills beside the rivers and Kingsbridge Estuary so that the wood could be transported by water.

SAWMILL AT GOODSHELTER, East Portlemouth, c. 1880.

SALCOMBE BOATYARDS, c. 1900.

DATE'S BOATYARD, Kingsbridge.

KINGSBRIDGE ONLY HAD ONE BOATYARD, Date's at New Quay. Between 1837 and 1912 it built over 85 vessels.

A SAWBENCH AT THE TIMBER YARD on Squares Quay, Kingsbridge.

MR WOODMASON, basket maker of Duke's Mill, Aveton Gifford. He cultivated osier beds in marshy valleys and made willow baskets of varying shapes for carrying produce on the farm and to market. Cut willow was stacked in a stream until the stakes could be stripped of their bark and then the 'withies' were dried in the sun to whiten.

LIDSTONE'S FOUNDRY, Duke Street, Kingsbridge. This was the largest of several foundries in Kingsbridge. From 1739 it made sheep shears and other agricultural tools. In the nineteenth century the foundry made chains and brass fittings for Date's vessels. Nearly every house in the district had a 'Lidstone', as the small cast-iron ranges were known; marked railings and drain covers can still be found in the streets. The foundry was destroyed by bombing in 1943.

MILLING. Every small river had several mills along it, unfortunately few were photographed. When the Abbot of Buckfast founded his new town at Kingsbridge in the thirteenth century he built a corn mill at the head of the estuary where it could be powered by both tide and leats. In 1798 that mill was converted to making woollen cloth and then, in 1845, it changed back to corn. The Trant family (above in 1895) were the last to run the mill which closed down in 1967 and was demolished in 1984.

WASHABROOKE MILL, Dodbrooke, Kingsbridge.

LODDISWELL MILL, postmarked 1903.

THE INTERIOR OF KELLANDS BREWERY in Church Street in c. 1900. In the eighteenth century malt was a major export from Kingsbridge and barley was exported in 'quantities scarcely to be credited' from Salcombe. Gradually two breweries took over from the inns' own brewhouses: the London Brewery in Church Street (later the Phoenix and Kellands) and the South Devon Brewery in Fore Street (later Prowses in Union Road).

SECTION SIX

Fishing

Every coastal village supplemented its income by fishing, some more successfully than others. All suffered, along with most Cornish villages, from the dramatic decline in pilchard shoals in the 1850–70s – probably due to over-fishing. During the latter half of the nineteenth century many villages turned to crabbing instead, but larger vessels still went out from Salcombe.

THE FISH MARKET at Normandy Way, Salcombe. 1904.

A FISHERMAN AVOIDS GETTNG HIS FEET WET at Hope Cove in around 1906. Hope Cove was famous for pilchard fishing in the early nineteenth century.

Harbour Mouth, Bantham

Valentines Series

THE AVON IS STILL A GOOD RIVER FOR SALMON; the Lords of the Manor of Aveton Gifford built a salmon trap further upstream in the sixteenth century. Notice the semi-derelict fish quay in the shelter of the sandspit; the hut has since been rebuilt.

FISHERMAN JOHN KING lived in a cottage on Wonwell Beach, Bigbury.

IVY COVE, Lannacombe. Any small cove could be used to beach boats. Lannacombe was so secluded that there were rumours of smuggling too.

THIS PICTURE IS SIMPLY LABELLED 'CAMP OF COLLAPIT'. He was crossing Tacket Wood Bridge on the old Salcombe road. *Circa* 1900.

FISHING GROUP ON THE SALTSTONE, C. 1890. To many local people fishing was a recreation. This family group have gone to the Saltstone for a day out. They took their laundry tub to hold the fish! The Saltstone, in the middle of Kingsbridge Estuary, is only uncovered at low tide and is outside any parish boundary. It was the site of non-conformist services during the seventeenth century when they were illegal on the mainland.

BEESANDS FISHERWOMEN in 1898. The Cookworthy Museum's photographic collection is particularly rich in pictures of the Start Bay crab fishery.

The earliest documentary evidence for fishing in Start Bay comes from 1309 when the lord of the manor of Stokenham demanded that his bondsmen should fish for mullet with their own boats and tackle. He then took one third of their catch or its selling price.

By the nineteenth century net fishing was part of a sequence. First 'seining' for soft fish such as mullet or mackerel which were used as bait for the 'longlines'. Longlines were laid near the sea bed; from them hung twelve short lines with baited hooks to catch 'firmer' fish suitable for baiting the crab pots.

HALLSANDS, between 1904 and 1917. The southernmost village of Start Bay was Hallsands. Huddled below the cliff, its protective shingle beach removed by gravel dredging, the village was finally destroyed by a storm in 1917. The uncomfortable site was probably chosen because it was good for spotting shoals of fish as they travelled along the coast.

HALLSANDS, pre-1899, showing the original width of beach before the builders of Devonport Dockyard began to dredge off-shore for shingle to make concrete.

The beaches of Start Bay are golden shingle. There are no natural harbours but the broad expanse of pebbles was used to beach fishing boats out of reach of the highest tides.

BEACHING BOATS at Beesands, c. 1900.

HALLSANDS, 1900. Women prepared fish, hauled up boats and nets and carried their menfolk to the boats so that they didn't start the day with wet feet.

TUCK SEINING AT HALLSANDS. *Circa* 1896. A 'hillman' kept watch from the cliffs for a dark shadow on the sea which indicated a shoal of fish coming along the shore. The seine boat crew rowed gently round the shoal, paying out weighted nets until they got back to the shore. When the fish were surrounded, the arms of the net were hauled in trapping the fish in the centre or 'bunt'.

BEHIND THE BOYS AT HALLSANDS is a longline catch being dried for crab bait.

CRAB POTS were made of willow by the boat crews – the farmers who owned the osier beds were paid in fish. The pots were baited with fish stuck on a hazel twig down the funnel and weighted with stones before being laid on the sea bed.

SALE OF LOCAL CRABS ON KINGSBRIDGE FAIR DAY, outside the White Hart, Kingsbridge, c.1890. Before the First World War a 'crab smack' came from Southampton to the Start Bay villages every couple of weeks. The crabs were kept alive in a well in the vessel.

START POINT LIGHTHOUSE, C. 1900. When built in 1834, the lighthouse consisted of a single round tower with a revolving light on top; the keepers lived below the light. The original machinery operated until 1871–4 when a new lantern was installed along with other improvements and additions. Today the Start light is visible for over 21 miles. The Start has always been a good vantage point. Legend has it that local inhabitants watched the defeat of the Spanish Armada from here in 1588.

ONE OF THE HOPE COVE LIFEBOATS, the *Alexandra*. The Salcombe Lifeboat committee decided they needed a new station on the far side of Bolt Tail. The Earl of Devon gave the land at Hope and the house was funded and built by the Freemasons as a thanksgiving for the recovery from illness of Edward, the Prince of Wales. The first boat was named *Alexandra* after his wife. It was the first of four to bear the name, being replaced in 1887, 1900 and 1903. The station closed in 1930 when a motorised lifeboat was introduced at Salcombe.

LESTY, SALCOMBE LIFEBOAT from 1887–1904. The South Sands lifeboat house was built in 1878.

SECTION SEVEN

Childhood

WEST ALVINGTON SCHOOL, 1895. 'From top left-hand corner: Alf Edgecombe, ? Voysey, Mildred Hyne, Edie Moore, Victor Hyne, Will Moore, Sam Goss. Fred Edgecombe, Percy Barnes, Henry Hill, Frank Reeves, Bessie Cole, Francis Ingram, Katie Whiteway. Clara Voysey, Edgar Sandover, Crystal Luckham, Lizzie Ingram, Bertha Reeves, Fred Lidstone, Mable Gillard. Albert Reeves, ? Voysey, Frank Gillard, Albert Rich, Ella Rich, Freda Whiteway, Elsie Cole, Charlie Rich. Headmaster: Mr Denton.'

CHILDREN CLIMBING THE STILE AT TUMBLY HILL. A steep lane between Ropewalk and Square's Quay, Kingsbridge, Tumbly Hill was a convenient way for carriers to evade the tolls charged at the turnpike gate at the bottom of West Alvington Hill. The houses were compulsorily purchased in 1972 and stood derelict for around fifteen years.

WEST CHARLETON SCHOOL GROUP.

YARMER BEACH, Thurlestone, between 1903 and 1909.

KINGSBRIDGE GRAMMAR SCHOOL, 108 Fore Street, in c. 1875. Founded in 1671 by Thomas Crispin, the school took boarders, fee paying pupils and scholarship boys. The first headmaster was William Duncombe who left money in his will to set up various local charities; Duncombe Street was named after him.

GRAMMAR SCHOOL BOYS, c. 1880. Back row: Pullen, Cove, Brooks, Mr Dawson, Troake 1, Langworthy, May, Adams, Mr Molesworth, Gale, Sparrow, Honck, Fairweather, Mr Cloutte. Middle row: Allen 1, Hooper, Langworthy, Coker, Cox, Troake 2, Lys, Rundle 2, Lamble, Coker ?, Adams, Allen 2. Front row: Adams, Stoneman, Crimp, Steer, Swindenbank, Spear, Rundle 1, Wakeham, and Cloutte's dog – Caesar.

AN OLD KINGSBRIDGIAN, W. H. SQUIRE, noted cellist and composer, on the afternoon of his first public engagement in February 1879 at the Town Hall, Kingsbridge.

THE BOARD OF EDUCATION criticised the Grammar School premises in 1911 and the school spread into various other buildings in the town, primarily to 20 Fore Street seen here.

THE SEVENTEENTH-CENTURY SCHOOLROOM still provided school meals, and the rest of the building housed dormitories, kitchens and the headmaster's household.

ONE OF THE CLASSROOMS.

THE NEW GRAMMAR SCHOOL finally opened at Kingsley Road in 1931. Since 1971 the Old Grammar School has been the home of the Cookworthy Museum.

TWYFORD SCHOOL HOCKEY TEAM, 1911. R. Blackler, K. Langworthy, C. Harris, M. Balkwill, E. Irish, K. Coyte. E.M. Balkwill, A. Hannaford, A. Prettyjohn, K. Pascoe.

Twyford House (now Quay House) was a private school for girls. It ran into staffing difficulties and became part of the Grammar School in 1944. The girls remained at Twyford House until 1950 when new classrooms were built for them at Kingsley Road. The school did not became truly mixed for several years.

SUNDAY SCHOOL OUTING to Torcross, 1913.

FOR WOMEN, THE NATURAL CAREER WAS STILL, ULTIMATELY, MARRIAGE. Until then many went into service or worked in shops. Every young country woman had to know how to run the dairy – these young ladies are competitors in a butter-making class at Kingsbridge Fair. The tent flaps are raised to keep the cream at the correct temperature so that it will 'turn'.

SECTION EIGHT

Celebrations

QUEEN VICTORIA'S GOLDEN JUBILEE OF 1887.
'The public dinner was laid out in Ebrington Street where about one thousand sat down to the good things provided . . . 1000 lbs of beef; 50 lbs of pork; 3 bags of new potatoes; 480 lbs of bread; 715 lbs of plum pudding; 48 bottles of pickles (also salt and mustard); 72 gallons of beer; 10½ gallons of cider; 20 dozen large bottles of lemonade; and 37 dozen of ginger beer.'
Kingsbridge Gazette, 1887.

'Perhaps the most ingenious of the trade displays was the 'Vineyard Trophy' sent by Mr P. O. Hingston. This consisted of an enormous representation of a bottle of champagne, so arranged as to dip at the arches. At intervals the cork of this bottle was removed and a clear and sparkling liquid was noticed to fizz up into the sunlight.'
(Report in the *Kingsbridge Gazette*, 1887)
P. O. Hingston was a Wine and Spirit merchant at 8 Mill Street.

THE FIREWORK COMMITTEE, 1887. Written on the back is: 'Centre figures: Mr Harry Prowse, Ped Nicholls; Mr Pope, with moustache; Harry Square (white cap); extreme left, Johnnie Carpenter; next, Mr Mignot Tucker (chemist), next, J. R. Gill'

THE 1897 JUBILEE CELEBRATIONS outside 80 Fore Street.

MR JARVIS AND THE STEAR FAMILY (saddlers in Duke Street, Kingsbridge) in fancy dress for a procession to celebrate the coronation of Edward VII in 1901.

THE FASHIONS AND 'GOD SAVE THE KING' BANNER indicate that this must be the procession to celebrate the coronation of Edward VII in 1901. The 'decorated bicycle' class has sadly lapsed in more recent carnivals, and this must have been a monster street tea!

TOWN HALL, Kingsbridge. The official proclamation of George V as King. In the days before newspapers all important events were announced by the Town Crier in the main streets. After the Town Hall was built in 1850 proclamations were made from its steps. Notice the crowd of Grammar School boys in the centre.

GEORGE V's CORONATION DAY, Aveton Gifford. 1910.

A STREET PARTY IN EBRINGTON STREET to celebrate King George and Queen Mary's Silver Jubilee. 1935.

KINGSBRIDGE CARNIVAL 1929. The drinking fountain was erected to commemorate Queen Victoria.

MILL STREET, Kingsbridge. Either George V's Silver Jubilee in 1935 or possibly VE Day.

1908 SALCOMBE CARNIVAL. 1 – ? –, 2 – Beatrice Harnden, 3 – Bessie Arundel, 4 – Stella Pearce, 5 – ? –, 6 – Ethel Lapthorne, 7 – ? –, 8 – Edith Harnden.

THESE FIREWORKS OVER SALCOMBE HARBOUR ON REGATTA NIGHT were photographed in c. 1930 by a keen amateur photographer, Alwyn Staddon, whose father ran a boot and shoe shop at 75 Fore Street, Kingsbridge from 1906 until 1943.

SECTION NINE

Leisure and Holidays

The arrival of a circus or fair was a rare excitement; for the most part entertainment was 'home grown'. There were educational societies, like the Literary and Scientific Institute, and many others whose purpose was entirely recreational. Since the opening of the Town Hall with its small theatre there has been a continuous tradition of amateur dramatic and operatic productions.

Tourists began to visit the area in the mid-nineteenth century, attracted by the much-advertised 'salubrious climate'. Salcombe developed early but Hope Cove, Thurlestone and Torcross rapidly caught up. From 1893 the railway brought greater numbers of regular visitors as far as Kingsbridge and local entrepreneurs were not slow to provide charabancs and coaches to transfer them to their village destinations.

THE DEVONSHIRE ASSOCIATION at the Bolt Head Hotel in around 1900.

THE LAPTHORNES on a family outing to Bantham.

KINGSBRIDGE PISCATORIAL SOCIETY began as a successful joke with a series of humorous articles in the Kingsbridge Gazette. Its members, mostly local business men, went tuck seining in the Estuary creeks and gained as much satisfaction from duckings as from fishing.

SALCOMBE RUGBY FOOTBALL CLUB'S ANNUAL DINNER at Cliff House, 20 May 1948.

1923–24 BEESANDS ROVERS FOOTBALL TEAM with their lucky horseshoe posing before the Cricket Inn at Beesands. Their pitch is so close to the sea that rivals claim they have to check the tide tables before arranging a fixture.

TWO VIEWS OF A FUN FAIR on the Quay at Kingsbridge. They are difficult to date but could be c. 1880. The photographer had access to the garden and upper rooms of Ryeford House which used to stand on the site of the large supermarket at the foot of Fore Street. Behind Hurford's Kaffirs (a challenge wrestling booth?) the white building was Boon's coach works.

THE PLEASURE FAIR.—As usual the lower part of the town and Mr. Beer's Quay were devoted to the pleasure fair. There were about the usual number of standings, shooting galleries, &c., but several things were conspicuous by their absence, and altogether the fair was not so large as usual. Purchase's unique collection of wax works receives a fair amount of patronage, and is of a higher and better class than usual. There are several groups of especial merit, particularly the judgment of Solomon, founded on 1 Kings III, Daniel in the Lion's Den, from Daniel VI., and the group of the Royal Family. Our readers will do well to avail themselves of this treat, which is seldom to be obtained in Kingsbridge.

1878

ARTHUR HARRIS as Samuel in the *Pirates of Penzance,* an Operatic Society production in the Town Hall.

FAMILY MUSICIANS, c. 1885.

D U P R E Z   I S   C O M I N G !
D U P R E Z   I S   C O M I N G !
D U P R E Z   I S   COMING!
D U P R E Z   I S   COMING!
DUPREZ   IS   COMING!
DUPREZ IS COMING!

The Greatest PRESTIDIGITATEUR the World
ever Saw.
Town Hall,
Wednesday, February 16th, Modbury, 17th.

DUPREZ IS COMING!
DUPREZ IS COMING!
D U P R E Z   I S   C O M I N G !
DUPREZ   IS   COMING!
D U P R E Z   I S   C O M I N G !
1878   **D U P R E Z   I S   C O M I N G !**

AVETON GIFFORD RECTORY.

CROQUET ON THE LAWN at Modbury Vicarage.

WHITEHALL, CHURCHSTOW, C. 1909. Described in 1866 as a 'fine mansion' its owners rarely lived here and it was tenanted. In recent years it was briefly a restaurant before being converted into luxury homes.

THE KITCHEN GARDEN AT WIDDICOMBE HOUSE, Torcross in the late 1930s.

COMBE ROYAL. South Devon's mild climate is favourable to gardens. Aloes grow and flower at Salcombe. Combe Royal oranges (grown outdoors in the alcoved wall in the lower picture) were sent to Queen Victoria in the 1860s 'who afterwards sent her head Gardener from Osborne for the purpose of enquiring on the spot as to the mode of culture.' (Fox, 1864)

MEET OF THE SOUTH POOL HARRIERS at Buckland House, Buckland Tout Saints.

To Masons, Carpenters, Plumbers, Painters and Glaziers, and others.

PERSONS desirous of tendering (separately) for the above branches of work, or in one sum for the whole of the works, proposed to be carried out in ALTERING and REPAIRING

BUCKLAND HOUSE,

Near Kingsbridge, South Devon, can inspect the Drawings and Specifications at my Offices in Kingsbridge. Further particulars can be obtained on application to E. APPLETON, Esq., Architect, Kingswear and Torquay, South Devon.

Tenders, endorsed "Buckland House," are to be delivered or sent to me, on or before SATURDAY, the 27th day of APRIL next.

The lowest or any Tender will not necessarily be accepted, and no payment will be made for any Tender submitted.

JNO. H. SQUARE,
Solicitor, KINGSBRIDGE.

Kingsbridge, 29th March, 1878.

1878.

COURTENAY WALK, Salcombe, c. 1875. Courtenay Walk was opened as a public cliff walk to Bolt Head by Lord Courtenay, later Earl of Devon, in the 1850s. This was a direct response to Salcombe's growing fame as a holiday venue.

SPLAT COVE, Salcombe. These three photographs were all taken by 'Mrs. Haynes, Artist, 40 Fore Street, Kingsbridge'. She took over her husband's photographic business and produced good quality views in the 1870s and 1880s.

BOLT HEAD. Here Mrs Haynes has arranged her figures to resemble a romantic painting.

BOLT HEAD TEA GARDENS below Courtenay Walk.

SALCOMBE FROM EAST PORTLEMOUTH.

From 1908 a GWR bus service ran from Kingsbridge Station to Salcombe. The York Hotel is now the Salcombe Hotel in Fore Street, Salcombe.

THURLESTONE BAY before the development of housing. Postmarked 1911.

ROYAL SANDS HOTEL, SLAPTON, SOUTH DEVON.

WAREHOUSES OR 'CELLARS' existed where Slapton Bridge road meets the Line from at least 1737. There were stores, a lime kiln and cottages and, by 1831, a public house which became the Sands Hotel.

THE ROYAL SANDS HOTEL, Slapton Sands. 'The Sands Hotel which is greatly frequented by gentlemen-fishers, although very pleasant in fine weather, must be comfortless indeed during the winter months, being built quite on the beach, and in fact, it is often during severe south-easterly gales (like the houses at Torcross) washed by the spray and invaded by the waves.' (Fox, 1864)

IN 1850 TORCROSS WAS DESCRIBED AS 'A PRETTY LITTLE BATHING PLACE' but by 1889 it warranted the description of 'a small watering place'. The Torcross Hotel built an extension in 1884 linking it to the two-storied building behind the boat.

HOLIDAYS AT HALLSANDS

with PATIENCE and ELLA TROUT

who own and *personally* manage Trout's Hotel
(formerly Prospect House Hotel)

TWO MODERN GARAGES *and ample free Parking space*

THE TROUT FAMILY were made homeless by the storm which destroyed Hallsands in 1917. They moved to Bickerton where the two eldest daughters worked on the farm in summer and fished in the winter. Later in 1917 Ella rescued a crewman from a torpedoed cargo ship in Start Bay; his family gave her a small gift of money which enabled the sisters to build a guest house, known as Prospect House. By 1933 it was enlarged and known as Trout's Hotel catering for up to 68 guests.

THE GARA ROCK HOTEL started life as a row of single-storey coastguard cottages, here seen in c. 1907. Later, (opposite page), a second storey was added and the ground floors extended.

GARA ROCK HOTEL, *opp.* SALCOMBE.

THE DEVELOPMENT OF THE GARA ROCK HOTEL.

GOLF CLUB AND LINKS, Thurlestone, *c.* 1900. Thurlestone Golf Club was founded in 1897 with the entrance fee 10*s.* 6*d.* and the annual subscription one guinea. There was a modest club house from the start – the veranda was added in 1899, the same year that the club appointed a professional. Other additions have been made through the years – tennis courts were opened in 1905 and the nineteenth hole was added in 1964.

GOLF CLUB AND LINKS, Thurlestone, *c.* 1905.

GOLF CLUB AND LINKS, Thurlestone, *c.* 1910? Notice the development of 'superior dwellings' around the village overlooking the course.

THE OPENING OF BOLBERRY GOLF LINKS in July 1907. The club house is now the Port Light Hotel.

MIXED BATHING AT HOPE COVE, postmarked 1913. Notice that the harbour wall has not yet been built.

SECTION TEN

Bad Times

FUNERAL AT MODBURY. In Kingsbridge the funerals of prominent citizens were awarded a particular mark of respect by local tradesmen. Blackened boards 'like floorboards' were fixed vertically across the centre of each shop window using catches left there for the purpose. After the funeral they were rapidly taken down again and returned to the store.

IN 1837 KINGSBRIDGE WAS MADE THE HEADQUARTERS OF THE LOCAL POOR LAW UNION which included 26 parishes. Some small village almshouses and poorhouses were kept for outworkers but most of them were closed. The poor, sick and insane from an area of over 113 square miles were sent to the newly built workhouse in Union Road. The accommodation, medical care and education may have been a slight improvement on what paupers had before, but they lost independence and village life. Parting from family and friends made the workhouse a place to be avoided if possible.

THE INMATES OF KINGSBRIDGE WORKHOUSE. Probably around 1910.

THE WORKHOUSE (upper left building) was built well away from the town. This picture was probably taken after the Great Blizzard of 1891.

Kingsbridge Cottage Hospital.   *Published by Bailey & Flower.*

KINGSBRIDGE COTTAGE HOSPITAL was first proposed as a suitable commemoration of Queen Victoria's Jubilee in 1887. It was finally opened in Duncombe Street on 2 April 1898 and closed in 1928 when it moved to new premises in Plymouth Road, now called the South Hams Hospital (below).

THE KINGSBRIDGE BARRACKS, AS THEY WERE IN 1812.

KINGSBRIDGE BARRACKS, 1812. During Napoleon's reign the fear of invasion was so great that in 1804 a military encampment was built on the east side of the estuary. It held up to 600 men and was only dismantled when Napoleon was defeated in 1815. Although they stayed such a short time the soldiers caused quite a stir amongst the small population – Ebrington Street was renamed Barrack Street for a while and a tavern called the Military Arms opened.

THE BATTERY AT SALCOMBE. Established in 1861, the battery above Fort Charles was manned by the Tenth Devon Artillery Volunteers (Salcombe). The two cannon were removed in the early 1900s.

SOLDIERS OF KINGSBRIDGE FIFTH HAYTOR BATTALION DEVON REGIMENT VOLUNTEERS on exercises on Salisbury plain. Back row: Cpl. Farr, Butcher T. Lidstone, Colour Sergeant Heavens, John Tanner, Hannaford (baker). Front row: Claude Stear, Hannaford, Bert Tanner. *Circa* 1902.

FORE STREET, Salcombe. Volunteers enlisting for the First World War.

SOME OF THE 'KING'S OWN' REGIMENT. 1914–1916.

SELLING HORSES AT AVETON GIFFORD. Written on the back is: 'Picture taken 7 August 1914. Horses had to be sold by Government order, they were needed to pull gun carriages in 1914–18 War. Poor things. In the picture are my father and grandfather Sandover, Mr Charles Luckraft of Challonscombe, Mr Walter Crimp of Tuffland (?), Mr Bowden of Titwell, Mr George Torring of Ashford, Dr Billie Steer and Uncle Jim Friend.'

Mr J. Pearce, of 8 Fore Street, witnessed the sale at Kingsbridge Quay on 6 August 1914, and wrote: 'Between 800 and 900 horses were brought for the inspection of the Army Authorities on the declaration of War by England on Germany. A large number were purchased. Never were there such a number of horses seen in Kingsbridge within living memory, extending in double lines up to the end of Ilbert Road, down the quay to the end of the Promenade and up to Market Place. Horses of every description, carriage horses, hunters, hacks, light and heavy brought. It being early closing day, shops were shut and everybody turned out to see such a sight. I saw 56 splendid animals being entrained at Kingsbridge Station for Bulford Camp, Salisbury Plain, in the best of condition, to be trained for heavy Field Artillery before being sent to the continent.'

SELLING HORSES FOR THE WAR on the Quay, Kingsbridge. 6 August 1914.

THE QUAY, Kingsbridge. 6 August 1914. The loss of so many horses had a serious effect on small farms.

PEACE SUNDAY, 20 July 1919. A united thanksgiving service in the Park at Salcombe.

TWYFORD SCHOOL FLOAT in the procession for Peace, 1919.

KINGSBRIDGE WAS HIT BY TIP AND RUN RAIDERS returning from bombing Plymouth. One bomb passed right through the new school buildings in Westville in the Christmas holidays of 1943, exploding in Kingsley Road.

KINGSBRIDGE HOME GUARD, c. 1940. Back row: Norman Tucker, Ralph Ball, Harold Ellis, Reg Hammett, George Weevil, Roy Giles, Cecil Rogers, Roy Richards, Claude Solomon, Bill Rogers, Fred Stephens, Oscar Quantock, Claude Luscombe, Norman Prowse, Simon Tucker. Middle row: Walter Court, Hubert Way, Les Cowler, Bill Jordan, Jack Foale, Bob Foxworthy. Front row: Bill Sidenham, Ned West, Eli Edgecombe, Tom Garnett, Herbert Marshall, Captain Saddler, Sergeant McCanless, Frank Gloyn, George Kellard, Harry Thoroughgood, Jack Tucker, Wilf Horswell. (Names provided by Jack Foale.)

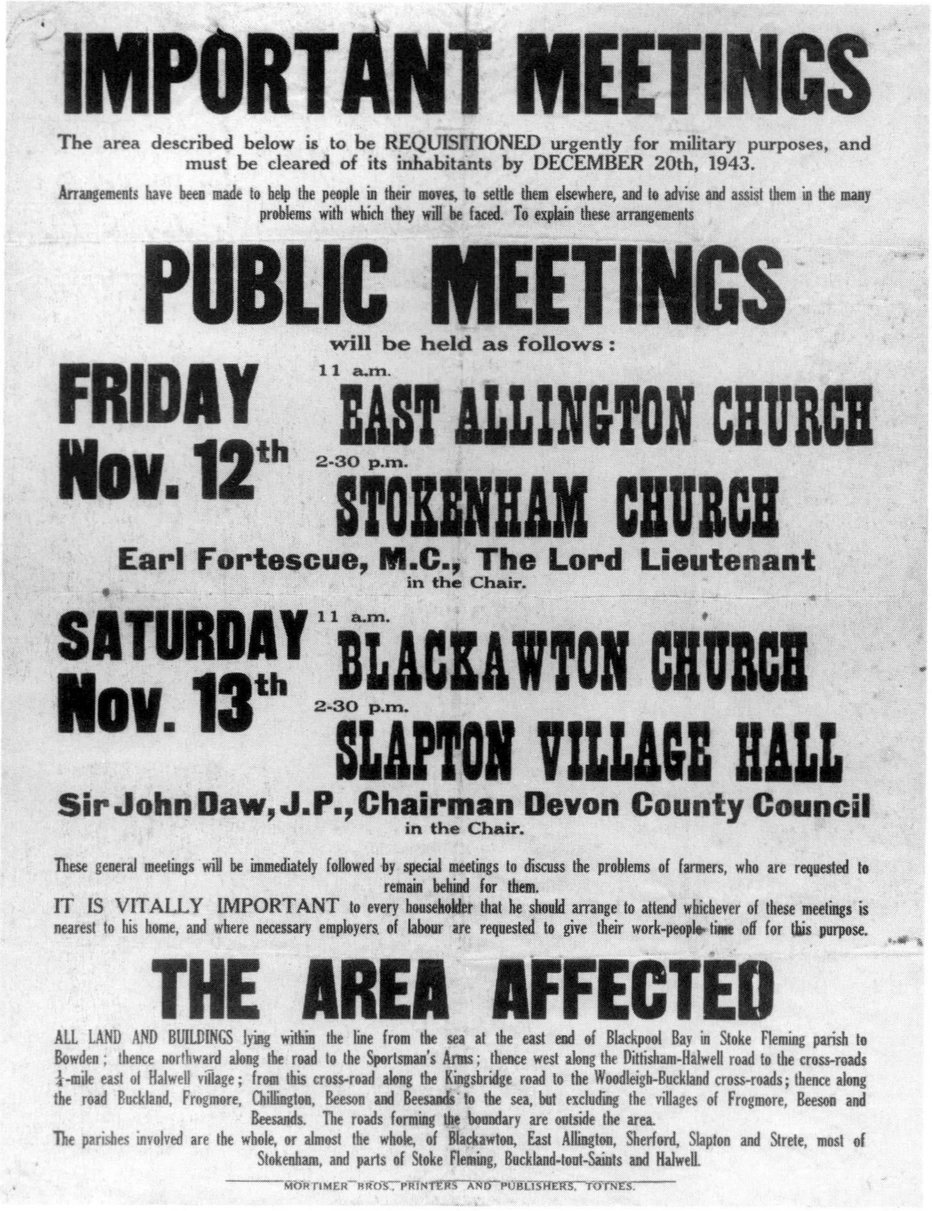

IMPORTANT MEETINGS

The area described below is to be REQUISITIONED urgently for military purposes, and must be cleared of its inhabitants by DECEMBER 20th, 1943.

Arrangements have been made to help the people in their moves, to settle them elsewhere, and to advise and assist them in the many problems with which they will be faced. To explain these arrangements

PUBLIC MEETINGS

will be held as follows:

FRIDAY Nov. 12th

11 a.m. **EAST ALLINGTON CHURCH**

2-30 p.m. **STOKENHAM CHURCH**

Earl Fortescue, M.C., The Lord Lieutenant in the Chair.

SATURDAY Nov. 13th

11 a.m. **BLACKAWTON CHURCH**

2-30 p.m. **SLAPTON VILLAGE HALL**

Sir John Daw, J.P., Chairman Devon County Council in the Chair.

These general meetings will be immediately followed by special meetings to discuss the problems of farmers, who are requested to remain behind for them.

IT IS VITALLY IMPORTANT to every householder that he should arrange to attend whichever of these meetings is nearest to his home, and where necessary employers of labour are requested to give their work-people time off for this purpose.

THE AREA AFFECTED

ALL LAND AND BUILDINGS lying within the line from the sea at the east end of Blackpool Bay in Stoke Fleming parish to Bowden; thence northward along the road to the Sportsman's Arms; thence west along the Dittisham-Halwell road to the cross-roads ¼-mile east of Halwell village; from this cross-road along the Kingsbridge road to the Woodleigh-Buckland cross-roads; thence along the road Buckland, Frogmore, Chillington, Beeson and Beesands to the sea, but excluding the villages of Frogmore, Beeson and Beesands. The roads forming the boundary are outside the area.

The parishes involved are the whole, or almost the whole, of Blackawton, East Allington, Sherford, Slapton and Strete, most of Stokenham, and parts of Stoke Fleming, Buckland-tout-Saints and Halwell.

MORTIMER BROS., PRINTERS AND PUBLISHERS, TOTNES.

THE BEACH AT SLAPTON SANDS closely resembled the proposed D-Day landing area in Normandy. In order for our American allies to use it as a battle training ground the beach and hinterland were completely cleared. Over 3,000 residents were evacuated during November and December 1943.

THE LAST ROUND BEFORE EVACUATION OF THE KINGS ARMS, Strete. The landlord, Mr Britnell, was on a 48-hour leave from the navy. December 1943. (Torquay Natural History Society.)

MR E. HANNAFORD clearing his butcher's shop. (Torquay Natural History Society.)

MR F. LIFE, verger for 22 years at St Michael and All Angels, Blackawton, removing the rood screen from the church for safekeeping during the evacuation. (Torquay Natural History Society.)

CHURCH HOUSE INN, Stokenham, after the exercises. During the exercises the foreshore was mined, bombed and shelled using live ammunition. During one of the training sessions German E-boats sank two landing craft with heavy losses.

Before people could move back into the demilitarized zone bomb disposal teams worked to make it safe and the WRVS mounted an enormous cleaning operation.

After the war a thanksgiving memorial was unveiled on the site of the Royal Sands Hotel which had been demolished during the exercises. It recognises the sacrifices made by local people in giving up their homes and livelihoods to help the war effort.

SALCOMBE HARBOUR provided good shelter for American vessels at Salcombe.

THE WAR MEMORIAL AT KINGSBRIDGE.

On 9 and 10 March, 1891, the South Hams experienced 'The Great Blizzard'. Hurricane force winds on Monday drifted heavy snow falls into the deep lanes. The winds dropped on Tuesday but the snow continued.

THE BLIZZARD IN SALCOMBE. It was not until Wednesday that 'the bright sunshine and the clear, crisp air afforded an opportunity to the photographers, both amateur and professional'. (Kingsbridge Journal, 1891.) Salcombe was completely cut off from Monday evening until Friday.

THE ROAD FROM KINGSBRIDGE TO SORLEY was blocked by 12ft. drifts and the coaches to Kingsbridge Road station at Wrangaton could not run for 17 days. Labourers building the Kingsbridge to Brent railway helped to clear the snow.

OFFIELDS, at Churchstow on 30 December 1927. Almost 50 men were needed to clear the road between Kingsbridge and Aveton Gifford.

HIGH TIDES AT SALCOMBE, postmarked 1909.

HALLSANDS VILLAGERS GATHER THEIR BELONGINGS after the disastrous storm of 1917 which finally destroyed the village.

TORCROSS, 1951. Was this damage, and more recent devastation in 1979, the legacy of shingle removal in Start Bay opposite Hallsands at the turn of the century? (Western Morning News)

THE BARQUE *HERZOGIN CECILIE* was built in Germany in 1902 as a sail-training vessel. In 1921 she was transferred to Finnish owners who used her for more mundane commercial cargoes. In 1936, carrying a cargo of grain from Port Lincoln to Ipswich, she foundered on the Ham Stone and drifted into Sewer Mill Cove. She lay there for seven weeks – there was some slight hope of recovery so the vessel was towed into Starehole Bay. But the grain was swelling and giving off gases which made it impossible to salvage. The *Herzogin Cecilie* finally sank in Starehole Bay.

ACKNOWLEDGEMENTS

The author and Cookworthy Museum are grateful to the following institutions for allowing photographs in their care to be reproduced here:
Devon Library Services, Torquay Natural History Society and the Western Morning News.